D1557077

Introduction

Welcome to the jungle! Becoming a stepmother can be one of the most challenging experiences in a woman's life. It can also be one of the most rewarding ones. It all depends on how you handle it.

You have met the man of your dreams. You are living your love story. But things get a little complicated as you also have an immediate family with his children from another woman. How hard can it be, you think? You will love them just because they are his children. Not so fast.

Every family's circumstances are different. There are numerous uncontrollable factors, which will inevitably affect your relationship with your step-children and your role in the new household. After reading this book, you will be better equipped for the inevitable obstacles.

The purpose of this guide is not that you follow all of the suggestions immediately. But to incorporate the concepts into your game plan. The best first step is to be prepared. Take it slowly. Some of these tips can be put into action right away. Others may cause you to re-think your plans. These guidelines can help you to not only survive this experience, but to thrive as well.

1

Don't Put Their Mother Down

This one is first for a reason. You should never talk negatively about your stepchildren's mother in front of them. There are no exceptions to this rule.

The last thing they want to hear is you speaking badly about their biological mom. No matter what she has said or done, keep your composure, and you will earn their respect in time.

If you need to vent, do it when the stepchildren are not around.

2

Be Patient

You should not expect miracles to occur quickly. Blended families usually do not become instantly happy. It can take some time for everyone to adjust.

But if you are patient and understanding with the stepchildren's needs, progress can and will be made over time.

3

Be The Adult

There may be times when the stepchildren seem unreasonable. Remember who the adult is in the relationship. You need to rise above it.

Their standards are probably rigid and may seem unfair. However, you are the adult. They are the children. When things start to get emotional, you must keep your composure.

4

Understand Their View

The stepmother is the "outsider" in the minds of the children. They might even resist you in the beginning.

Their perception is likely different than yours. They did not choose you. Their father did. Remember this during the difficult times.

As you make progress developing a good relationship with the children, this can change. Usually, it doesn't happen overnight though.

5

You Have To Earn It

Just because you are now the "mom" of the household, doesn't automatically mean your step-children will respect you. You have to earn their respect.

This starts with being there for them. Sometimes stepmoms never get the love from the kids, but they can still earn their respect. It may take some time, but it can happen.

6

Be Positive

Try to make the transition to the blended family a pleasant one for the stepchildren. There has probably been some difficult times for them, and they need a positive influence.

Creating a positive family environment for the children is a very important part of being a good stepmother. Be their ray of sunshine.

7

Be Consistent

The transition to having a new "mother" in their lives can be very difficult for many children. Your new children will need some stability in their lives.

They need to know you will be there for them, when they need you. Being consistent with your approach helps to facilitate this process. You can't be perfect, but you can be consistent.

8

Be Available

A stepmother should be accessible to her step-children. Being available whenever they need something will go a long way towards building a positive relationship.

They may feel isolated to some extent from their biological mom. It doesn't mean you are taking their mother's place, just filling in as needed. There is an important role in their lives for you.

9

Build Rapport

Building rapport with your stepchildren is a necessary step for all good stepmothers. You want to build a strong bond over time.

One suggestion is to come up with some one on one activities. It doesn't have to be something original, just something fun for them. Let them pick the activity. The important thing is that you spend time with them.

10

Communicate With Their Mother

Try to establish open lines of communication with their mother if at all possible. It may be uncomfortable at first, but it can work if you are proactive and sincere in your attempts to communicate effectively.

All you can do is your part in this process. If the biological mom won't participate, you can't force it. But it will make life a little easier on you if you can work together. You never know, you may actually like one another.

11

Keep Your Composure

Blended families sometimes have to deal with emotional outbursts. It is critical that you, as the adult, keep your composure if harsh words are thrown around.

The children will have strong feelings and may at times express them. If they say something hateful, don't respond with something you will regret. Be the voice of reason. Show some restraint. Be the one who diffuses the situation.

12

Accept That The Stepfamily is Different

Do not expect the stepfamily to be the same as a biological one. For starters, the stepfamily exists because the biological family didn't work.

Therefore, there is likely to be baggage brought into the new situation. Current and past relationships must be worked out over time. So be patient and supportive as the process evolves.

13

Put The Marriage First

As important as the children are, the marriage must be the first priority. This doesn't mean you should neglect the stepchildren. However, a stable and loving relationship with your partner can set a good example.

This may cause some initial resentment from the step kids, but as time goes on, a strong and lasting relationship between you and your partner will be a good thing for them as well. After all, they don't want to be uprooted again by another failed relationship .

14

The Stepchildren and Their Father

Encourage the stepchildren to have a good relationship with their father. Don't ever stand in the way of their relationship.

You shouldn't feel envious if they are close. You should feel fortunate that they have sustained the relationship through the previous break-up. This will help the stepchildren to accept you too. More on this later.

15

Like Them First

Don't think you will immediately fall in love with your stepchildren. You might, but it is also possible you won't. Love for your stepchildren usually takes time.

Work on liking them first. Try to look for the good in them and respect them. Give them their privacy, but don't neglect them.

16

Don't Obsess

A perfect relationship is never going to exist between you and your stepchildren. So don't obsess over it and try to be a perfect stepmom.

Perfect relationships don't even exist between parents and their biological children. However, a wonderful, unique adult and child relationship can be established with time and patience.

17

Take Time For Yourself

While your spouse is the priority, you still need to take care of yourself. You should participate in some of your own activities and hobbies.

A little time to yourself can help you appreciate being a wife and stepmother even more. The better you feel about yourself, the easier it will be to accept others.

18

Develop One On One Relationships

It is very important to establish a personal relationship with each stepchild. If you only have one, then spend some one on one time with him or her.

If you have more than one stepchild, take the time to spend alone time with each one. Be careful to give each child equal time though. You don't want to create any resentment for perceived inequalities.

19

Preserve The Trust

Trust is essential in all relationships. Whatever you do, don't ever break their trust in you. It can be very difficult to get it back.
Talk to them and respect their wishes.

If they ask you not to tell their father something they've shared with you, don't do it unless you feel he must know. In that case, be honest with them and explain why he has the right to know.

20

Accept Your Role

Accepting your role as a stepmother is not easy. It is a very fine line. You don't want to replace their mother, but you do need to serve as the household's mother.

Don't try to force anything to happen too soon. Patience, understanding, and perseverance will be rewarded in the long run.

21

Don't Play The Blame Game

All relationships have rough patches. Problems will arise, and solutions will be needed. Don't get into the blame game. Blaming someone doesn't solve anything.

You are not responsible for the misbehaviors of your stepchild. Show some understanding instead of blaming people. Remember you are the adult. Be the leader in peacemaking.

22

Encourage Respect and Understanding

Depending on the size of your new family, it may not be possible for everyone to be close. Although members of the stepfamily may grow to love each other, it is also possible that it won't happen for everyone.

Either way, as the stepmother, you should encourage everyone to show understanding and respect for other family members. You should set the example yourself.

23

Don't Have Unrealistic Expectations

Don't count on the new blended family to run smoothly from the beginning. There will likely be some issues that must be worked out.

Don't set unrealistic goals that can't be met or you will be setting yourself up for disappointment. Give it some time and progress can be made.

24

Give Them Some Time With Their Father

Don't feel left out if the kids want some alone time with their daddy. It may not be anything against you. But the bond they share with him should be protected.

If they are already separated from their mother, they may need a little extra attention from their father. If you expect that the kids will be more demanding of their father's time, you won't feel isolated. You should even encourage the stepchildren to spend some alone time with their father.

25

Let Their Daddy Give Them Attention

Make sure to be very understanding of the attention the kids want and need from their father. You may want him all to yourself, but be willing to share.

If they feel you are taking him away from them, it will cause additional problems. Until they realize that you're not competing with them, it will be a little more difficult.

26

Be Flexible

Contrary to what you may be thinking, this has nothing to do with being an acrobat. Although at times, you may feel like you need to be to survive being a stepmom.

You must be willing to sacrifice at times. The transition to step motherhood will require some major adjustments from you. The transition period is an especially difficult time on the children. Be cognizant of this by being flexible to their needs.

27

Respect the Primary Triangle

Don't feel threatened by the relationship between the children and their biological parents. It is quite natural for the children to want their parents back together.

Unless something inappropriate is going on, you should let them have their time together. Your husband will need to work together with his ex for the children's best interests. Don't let a little jealousy cause a new set of problems.

28

Lend a Helping Hand

Be willing to help the stepchildren whenever they need it. But be careful not to be too pushy.

By talking with them, you can develop an understanding for what they would like and expect from you.

There is a fine line between being too helpful and not helpful enough.

29

Just Be You

When the step kids finally realize that you're not trying to replace their mother, they'll probably start liking you for who you are. You don't have to try and be like their mother.

Remember you have a romance to enjoy. Their father likely picked you because of who you are, not because you remind him of his ex. So just be yourself.

30

Accept Them For Who They Are

Now that you know you should be yourself, you should also let the stepchildren be themselves. Each stepchild is unique in his or her own way. Don't try to change them as individuals.

This is not to be confused with correcting their bad behaviors. Don't blame the children for the mistakes their mother may have made. Encourage them to appreciate who they are.

31

Have a Date Night

Hire a babysitter and spend the night out with your husband every once in awhile. Just like the children may need some alone time with their dad, you too deserve some private time.

As long as you're not doing this too much, it can be a very healthy thing for your relationship with your spouse. Try to do this on a regular basis, such as once per week.

32

Go To Their School Activities

Whenever the children invite you to a school function, accept and attend. If the stepchildren are doing the inviting, this is a good sign that you are welcome.

If you haven't been invited to any functions, then communicate your interest to the child. Let them know you want to be there to support them as long as you are wanted there.

The worst case scenario is you don't get invited and don't attend because each side assumed the other wasn't interested.

33

Fairness is a Must

If you and your new spouse bring your own children into the relationship, make sure you treat everyone equally. Children's feelings can get hurt very easily if they perceive a parent or stepparent is treating a sibling with favoritism.

You should strive to provide an atmosphere of fairness, treating all children with equal love and care. This may not come easy, but it is necessary to prevent additional resentment.

34

Don't Push It

As a new stepmother, you probably are eager to quickly develop a positive relationship with the stepchildren. You must realize that it can be a slow process. So don't push it and try to force things to happen.

Start by being a friend to them. Give them some time to allow you inside their circle of trust. Let it develop naturally, and it will likely be a stronger bond.

35

Build a Strong Home Base

Children that have endured the demise of the parent's relationship are often in some pain. They need to feel secure that their lives aren't going to be torn apart again.

You can help by building a strong home base with an environment full of love and support for all family members. By being available to the children both physically and emotionally whenever they need someone to talk to, you can help them heal.

36

Set New Rules

A new set of rules will need to be established for the new household. There are different dynamics at work, so appropriate rules are needed.

Work with your partner to build new house rules and establish your own traditions. Then come up with a game plan. But before you start enforcing rules, you will want to read the next couple pages.

37

Game Plan For Discipline

It is very important to agree on a game plan for discipline with your partner. Then present a united front to the children.

Talk about discipline early on with your spouse so that you are on the same page. You may be surprised to learn that you have different ideas on how the rules should be enforced.

However, it's important to work out any differences ahead of time and stick to your plan.

38

Start Slowly With Discipline

Starting out, your role in the blended family should be one of an adult friend, but not the disciplinarian. The biological parent needs to be pro-active in enforcing the rules in the early stages of stepfamily life.

Don't let this make you feel powerless. You need to focus on building the relationship before assuming a disciplinarian role. Otherwise, you will be resented. As the relationship develops over time, you can gradually transition into this role.

39

Find Common Interests

One of the best ways to bond with a stepchild is to find an activity that they love and participate with them. Even if it is not something you enjoy, give it a try. You never know, you may discover a new interest for yourself.

You should also talk with your stepchildren about what they like to talk about. Discovering mutual interests can be fun for both of you.

40

Talk Time

Find some time each day to talk to each stepchild one on one. Even if it's just for a few minutes, this is time well spent. During this time, ask them about what's on their mind. Give them an opportunity to express how they are feeling.

You can also inquire about that special something that they love to talk about. Maybe it's a new boyfriend, rollerblading, or a school project. Whatever it is, just ask them open-ended questions and let them talk. Be a good listener. They will love it.

41

Choose Your Battles Carefully

Be careful not to be too critical. By letting some things go, you may feel like you are slacking. But it is possible that it will help your outlook and could even enhance your stepfamily relationships.

How important is it really that the dirty plate makes it into the sink? You can't fight them on everything or you will be perceived as a nag. But you still need to focus on the important stuff. Certain rules can never be broken without consequences.

42

Give Unconditionally

A good stepmother will attend to the needs of her stepchildren without expecting it to be reciprocated. At least not right away. The stepchildren are likely to be a little hesitant trusting in you, so be patient with them in this regard.

If you can give without expecting anything in return in the beginning, you might be pleasantly surprised at the progress that you will make. It is a good investment that can pay off down the road in the form of a stronger relationship.

43

Savor Some Victories

Occasionally, you should savor some small victories on your journey as a stepmom. There will be times that you will be frustrated, but there should also be some good times.

Whenever you experience a positive sign of progress, celebrate it. High five yourself. Don't assume the battle is over, but look at it like one victory in a long season.

44

Simplify

Whenever possible, simplify your life. You may be wearing many different hats, and at times it may seem overwhelming. So be sure to prioritize things and focus on the most important things.

If there are some activities that are taking up a lot of your time then it's time to re-evaluate. Rank the top ten most time consuming things in your life. Then rank them in importance. You should quickly see which ones could be eliminated, or at the very least reduced. This will allow you more time for the important stuff.

45

Don't Underestimate The Obstacles

A stepfamily is one of the most challenging types of family relationships. Each new day can present new battles. The road may seem filled with obstacles. You must be prepared for it.

The first step is understanding the challenges are real. Don't be lulled into a false sense of comfort if things go smoothly for awhile. That is not to say you shouldn't enjoy those times. However, blending a family is an ongoing struggle which will require you to be prepared.

46

Set Goals

As you navigate your way down the path of being a stepmom, you need to experience progress. To get started, you should set realistic goals in writing.

Start by brainstorming for twenty minutes by listing all of the things you would like to accomplish as a stepmother. Don't hold back. Just let the ideas flow. After you have filled the page (or two), eliminate any that are unrealistic. Then separate them into short (less than one year), intermediate (12-24 months), and long term (more than two years). You now have your goals.

Remember to look at your written goals every day as a way to remind yourself of the targets and to know when you have accomplished one.

47

Don't Change The Schedule

You may want to change the visitation schedule, but don't. The transition period of a blended family is difficult enough without changing more things around.

Any perceived attempt to alienate the mother is going to result in arguments between the biological parents. Guess who will get the blame for it? Yes, you, the stepmother.

This is a bad way to get things started. Even if the schedule is inconvenient, let Dad initiate any discussions about changes.

48

Don't Imitate Their Mom

As mentioned earlier, you must be yourself. Don't try to be like their mother. You may be thinking that's crazy. Why would I want to do that? If so, you get the point. If not, remember that you are not her. You are your own unique person.

The biological mother may be a wonderful person that they love dearly. That is okay. There is still room for you in their lives. Don't try to replace her. The children need you and her. They don't need her and an imitation.

49

Try To Be Friends

If you and the biological mother can work together, things will go much smoother. There are many stepmothers who have actually developed friendships with the mother. After all, you both have the children's best interests in mind.

If you can have a civil relationship, life will be so much easier. This may not be possible depending on the circumstances, but if it is, work towards it. The kids will be better off because of it.

50

Wait To Insert Yourself

When it comes to school related conferences, such as parent-teacher meetings, you should initially leave that to the biological parents. Until you have established a good relationship with your stepchild, you shouldn't barge into these situations. Doing so could create conflicts with their mother.

However, if circumstances are such that the mother can't or won't handle this responsibility, you should discuss a course of action with your spouse, such as having him handle it for awhile, then gradually introducing you into the role.

51

Put Yourself In Their Shoes

Perceptions are often reality. This is often true in blended family situations. Try to look at things from the children's perspective.

They may see you as trying to replace their mother. They may also see you as someone trying to replace them in their father's life. You may think that sounds ridiculous, but children may not.

By talking to your stepchildren and putting yourself in their shoes, you can gain a greater understanding of how they feel.

52

Take a Break

As you know by now, step mothering can be challenging stuff. It's important to recharge your batteries. Every once in awhile, take time to do things for yourself.

Go shopping with a friend, take a long walk, get a massage, read a romance novel, or whatever it is that you enjoy. It's a necessary step in keeping your sanity.

53

Keep It To Yourself

This is so important, it bears repeating. As step-mom, there may be many things you dislike about the ex-wife. Although this is a common feeling, you can not express that in front of the children.

Saying something negative in the presence of the children can create a great deal of animosity. The last thing they want to hear is this person who took their mother's place spouting off about their mom. In the stepchildren's minds, you are attacking them too, since they are made up of half of each parent.

54

Accept Your Role And Thrive

A stepmom is many things. She acts as a nurse but she rarely gets nurtured. She is a central figure in the household but rarely is the favorite. The list goes on and on.

As a matter of fact, it may seem like a thankless role at times. But any woman that can survive and thrive as a stepmom is to be commended. That person can be you. Believe in yourself.

55

Relax

Lastly, don't get upset when everything does not go as expected. It won't be perfect. But it can still be good. Relax a little.

Enjoy the good times, and learn your lessons. Treasure your marriage and work together to ensure a loving family household where the children feel secure.

Conclusion

There you have it... the 55 ways to be a better stepmother. Even after applying some of these suggestions, don't expect the stepfamily to run smoothly from the beginning. It takes time to develop common values, family history, and traditions.

Feeling comfortable and accepted as a stepparent might take years. It can also take months, or in rare cases, it can happen the day you enter the child's life. Whatever happens, most likely, your goal of respect will not come easily.

Don't assume you will be a good stepmother just because you are a good mother. They are two totally different situations. Although some qualities are necessary for both, there are many new challenges with being a stepmom.

Just remember that your stepchild may never love you like they love their parents. That's natural. But they can love you as the next best thing, and that's a pretty good thing.

Be prepared for a difficult battle. Apply the tips in this book and you will be on your way to being a good stepmother. Remember it's a marathon, not a sprint.

Made in United States
North Haven, CT
21 April 2022

18449770R00036